First

For

Me

2000-2003

Stephanie Jacobson

Printed in the United States of America.

Table of Contents

Table of Contents

Table of Contents

Table of Contents

buffalo

I should be back in Buffalo
Somewhere down on Main Street
Walking along
Watching the cars pass by
Wondering where everyone
Was going
In such a hurry

new year

A new day
A new year
A new me
Isn't that the way
It always is
You plan to make this year
Better than your last
Not to make the same mistakes
Not to have the same short-comings
Not to fall for the same tricks twice

trying to fool

Who are you
Trying to fool?
Any of you
All of you
You're all so pretentious
And fake
Your dyed hair
Your designer clothes
Your designer attitude
Your pagers and cell phones
Your fancy cars with
Remote alarms
Who have you impressed
But yourselves?

invisible

Do you people
Not see me
Sitting here?!
As you stare blankly
Through me
And wait for me
To move out of
Your way

no purpose

I feel as though
My life has no purpose
No meaning
Or fulfillment
Everyone else
Has got a steady job
With decent pay
Everyone else
Is going to college
Or already has
Some type of degree
Everyone else
Is moving out on their own
To have their own place
To call home
But me
I had eight and a half hours last week
I dropped out of college
And I still live at home

surprises

I don't like surprises
Never have
Never will
There's too much
Built up
To live up to
And then it's always
A let down
Because it didn't live up
To expectations

same old place

There's nothing you could do
To this place
To make it look appealing
To me
Unless you tore it down
And started
All over again
But the newness would
Only last so long
Before it just went back to
The same old place it was

happy

I feel like
I'm holding you back
From doing what
You want to do
From doing what makes
You happy
That you're only here
To absolve some guilt
Afraid of hurting me
I wonder if I should just
Bow out gracefully
Say good-bye
Leave you to live your life
The way you
Want to
Without me
So you can be
Happy

assholes

I don't understand
Why you people
Feel the need
To brag about
How fucking drunk
You got
How you didn't know
Where you were
Or how you got there
And that you were
Sick as a dog
For the rest of the day
In your attempt
To make yourselves
Sound cool to others
You're just making yourselves
Look like assholes

double zero

I'm not fond of this
Double-zero thing
For dating my pages now
It just doesn't look right
All those zeros
It looks empty
And cold
Up there in the corner
Of the page
The date
With it's double-zeros

in atlanta

After eleven years, it's over
And I find myself having
To start all over again
Here,
In Atlanta
Where we met
All those years ago
When I first saw you
Across the room
Your blonde hair glistened
In the light
And I lost myself in
Your soft, brown eyes
I fell in love with you
That instant
In Atlanta

over you

Snow falls outside
My window
As I sit alone
In a booth
In the back
Drinking my coffee
Fighting off sleep
My mind wanders
To the thought of you

tropics

I should be
Somewhere warm
On a white sandy beach
Near crystal blue waters
The warm tropical sun
Peering down at me

ravaged

My body feels ravaged
Beaten
Broken
And sore
I feel like I have
To fight
To keep my eyes open

aches & pains

My head aches
From caffeine withdrawal
My jaw aches
From infection
My back hurts
From bending over backwards
To please you people

secrets

Have you ever had a secret
You really wanted to tell
Somebody
For no other reason
Than to tell them
Because they know
Everything else
About you
Except for this
One thing
That would change
The direction
Of the conversations
From time to time

we

We're too alike
To be apart
Too different
To be together
And I'm stuck
Here in the middle
Of wanting you
And needing you
And wondering if
I should let go

he said

I trace the curve
Of your jaw
Lightly
With my finger
Drawing you
Into me
Closer and closer
Your soft lips
Press against mine
You lay back
Opening yourself up
To me
Hands embraced
Fingers interlocked
We raise our arms
Above your head
I let go
Fingertips dancing
Down
Down
Down your arms
Over your shoulders
Your skin
Soft and delicate
My tongue traces
The curve of your neck
I inhale you
Your scent
I taste you
The salt of your sweat
As my tongue

Descends
Down your body
Over the swell
Of your
Creamy white breasts
Still entrapped
In your black satin bra
My finger dances
Delicately
Down your stomach
Causing you to
Quiver slightly
Your breathing
Becomes heavier
As my tongue
Follows
My finger
Follows along
The band of elastic
On your black satin panties
And I continue my
Descent
Down your luscious body
Down your thighs
Your calves
I take your foot
Into my hands
Caressing
Touching
Taking each
Lovely
Painted toe
Into my mouth

One by one
You call out to me
Wanting me
Your eyes
Invite me
To seduce you
To take you
To love you…

all of me

You ask me
To give myself
To you completely
Everything
All of me
To be at
Peace
With you
With myself
And I give
Myself
To you
Completely
All of me
To be in love
With you

tonight

You look
So beautiful
Tonight
My dear
Your golden blonde
Locks
Cascading around
Your face
The candlelight
Dancing
In your
Soft brown eyes
Your smile
Captivates me
Intrigues me
And makes me
Want you

stolen moments

"I don't understand you
Sometimes"
I say to you
And settle back
Into the couch
You just smile
"What's there to understand?"
You ask
Tossing me a cold one
"You're simply complex…
Or complicatingly simple,
I'm not sure which."
I explain
"You're the one I
Don't understand,"
You respond
Looking deep into my eyes
"You have beautiful eyes, my dear"
I say
"And you're a good fuck"
You smile
As you straddle my hips
Loosening my tie
And pulling the band
Out of my hair
"Baby, are you sure
This is the right time
For this?"
"It's as good a time as any,"
You say
Before you kiss me

I want to take you
Right then and there
But I can't
Not under the circumstances
I pull away
Reluctantly
"The guys will be back
Any second,
My boy"
I remind you as
I run my hands
Across your back
Not wanting to stop
"That's what makes it all the
More exciting, my dear"
You tease,
Kissing my neck,
Unbuttoning my shirt,
Running a hand
Down my chest
I lean back,
close my eyes
and lose myself in you
"It's like I said before,
I just don't understand
You sometimes."

my bed

If I could just
Spend all of
My time
In my bed
I'd be so
Relaxed
All of my pillows
Around me
All snuggled in
Under my blankets
Comfy and warm

alone again

I watch you walk
Across the room
That familiar
Swagger
And that shit-grin
Of yours
I can't help but laugh
Partly because of how
Hard you're trying
Partly because I want you
You sit down
Across from me
And just stare
I have to remind myself
We're in a public place
And restrain myself
From reaching across the table
Grabbing you by your shirt collar
And shoving my tongue
Down your throat
Instead I smile
Put my arm around my girl
As you do the same to yours
And count the time
Until we can be
Alone again

amazing

"You
are
amazing"
I breathe heavily
Rolling onto my back
My heart pounding
Covered in a sheet of sweat
You rest your head
On my chest
And sigh deeply
I play with your dark curls
Never in all my
Wildest dreams
Did I think
I'd be here
And be
With someone like you
And yet not be able
To share this
With anyone else
Because of who we are

fuck this

Fuck this shit
I'm tired
And cold
And I wish I was
Home
Sound asleep
In my warm bed
I had things
I needed to do
Tomorrow
(actually, now, today)
It's seven o'clock
In the fucking morning
And I'll be lucky if I get
4 hours of sleep
Damn it!
But,
I smile and lie
When you ask me if I'm tired
And ask my opinion
On all of this stupid shit
It's daylight out now
And we're finally
Getting to bed
Fuck this

this pain

I think I'm gonna
Miss this pain
When it's gone
It's been part of me
For four days now
And I'm getting
Used to it
Maybe I'm a bit of a
Masochist
When it comes right
Down to it
Maybe it just gave me
Something new
To whine about

in common

I've come to realize
We don't have
All that much
In common
Anymore
And I find myself
Struggling
To fit into your world
I'm looking for
Some type of
Guidance
Some type of
Style and
Individuality
But find myself
Trying to conform
To you and your
ideals

alone

I'm tired of being alone
All the time
Even when I'm in the
Company of others
Like no one wants me
Around
I don't get invited
Out to do all the things
Everyone else does
I just hear about them
The next day
I don't think I'm
Asking too much
I just want to feel
Included
Part of something
Like a real friend

twenty-one

I'm 3 months away
From being 21
And thinking that's the
Magical number
That's going to change
My life somehow
Make me just a tad
More popular
A tad more respected
I'm treated like a
Little kid so often
That I almost forget
I'm not

this big act

I feel like I have to
Prove something to you
Put on this big act
So you won't be disappointed
I just don't know
Which act to play
Anymore

better

I feel I need to better myself
Some how
Some way
I should read more
And a broader range of
Information
I should get a better job
More professional

bullshit

Judge not, lest ye be judged yourself

Do unto others as you would have done unto you

Fuck that ignorant bullshit
It doesn't work anymore
Not in this day and age anyway
You can't walk down the street
Out of your house
Without someone saying something
Thinking something
About you
Your hair, your clothes, your personality
You do it to feel better
About your own situation
In life
By putting others down

What bullshit

respect

Don't fucking tell me about
Respecting you
"You don't give respect,
You don't get respect…
You better beat respect outta me, boy"
The more I go one
The more that phrase makes sense

today's young woman

I don't seem very feminine
As I raise my soapy leg
From the bath
And run the razor over
The stubble that's grown in
These past two days
I think some part of me
Has been conditioned as a
Woman to rid my body of hair
I run my hands over my upper thighs
Noticing some of my
Pale white stretch marks
Are turning purple
I think about tanning
But that would rid me of the
Pale skin you say you love
But the tanning would mask
The flaws of my skin
I begin to wonder why I
Started doing all of this in
The first place
This shaving deal;
As I move one to my
Underarms which never seem
To be shaved close enough
Then down my arms
The newest edition to my
Shaving regimen
I thought it would have a
Nice look
A nice feel to it

Bare, hairless, smooth arms
So now they get done, too
I ponder for a moment
Whether to pluck the few
Dark hairs below my naval
Or to shave them
Since the tweezers are too far away
I make a quick sweep with
The razor over them and they disappear
I continue my descent to my
Pubic hair and start off by
Trimming it into a nice little square
Above my clit
Decide the edges aren't even enough
And get rid of it all
Being careful not to nick
The delicate folds that make up
The outer petals of my
Womanly flower
I think about what you said
About me having nice nipples
And a comment about someone else's nipples
Slips back into my mind briefly
Enough to destroy what little idea
There was to me thinking my
Small breast weren't so small
After all
I turn on the hot water
To warm my bath again
Stirring the water with my foot
Letting the warm water dance
Over my bright pink painted toenails
I could easily slip under

The water
Inhale deeply
Filling my lungs with water
And cease to exist
But for some reason I think
I'm better off here
There's still things to be done
I day daydream
Wondering what it would
Be like living with you
If I would still take baths
And shave
While you sat there watching me
Telling me about all the other
Girls you know as I wonder
In my mind if they're better than me
I pull the plug and watch the water
Drain for a moment
Before standing up
A bit dizzy from the hot bath
Grabbing a towel and wrapping it around me
Being careful stepping out of the tub
I dry off, unclip my hair
That's been piled on top of my head all night
And stand in front of the full length mirror
Naked
Trying to see what you see
I think about putting
Thirty bucks aside for the
Gym this month to
Flatten my tummy
Firm up my hips and thighs
I play with my breasts

Pushing them up
Thinking maybe if I toned up my
Pecs they'd look better
I sigh
Wrapping myself in my
Bathrobe and succumbing to the society
Conditioned self-loathing
That is today's young woman

not dating

It's so hard to love somebody
Who says they don't love you back
Especially when you don't
Understand why
You're happy together
You name each other feel great
Neither of you want to see other people
And you're both jealous of the opposite sex
In the other's life

Yet...
You're not dating

split

Let's move in together
Live under the same roof
Come home to each other
Every night
Curl up together when we go
To bed
Pool our money and share
He expenses
I have nothing to hide form you
Except maybe that I love you
Although I think you know that
No matter how hard I try to hide it

jazz

Man,
Them cats can wail
And I'm pleasantly
Stuck here
Between a rock
And a cool place
If only there was a
Place to hang and chill in town
With a groovy jazz feeling
Where I can sit and relax
And somebody can wait
On me

working girl

I should go check on my tables
And see if these old ladies
Need anything else
Instead I'm standing here
Losing myself in some
Sweet Charlie Parker

at the diner

This is bullshit!
I can't believe the crap
Other people believe
I can't believe the
Amount of shit
Other people have to put up with
And how fucking annoying
It is to sit across from
The college kids who chew
Their food like cows chew their cud!
Bastards!
I'd love to be moved to that booth you just cleared
I'd love an ashtray
And a cup of coffee
While you're at it

here

I
Don't
Understand
How I ended up here
In this particular
Place in this particular life
What I did wrong
In the past
To end up with this
As my future

you say you don't

I hate the
Fact that you say you don't love me
When my heart aches
So much
For you
I wish there was something
I could do to
Change things
For you and I to be together
For you and I to live together
Sometimes I wonder
If it's me
You tell me how sexy
How attractive I am to you
How I make you happy
How you're comfortable with me
And how there's no one else
You want to be with
Except for someone else

better to do

It's not like I don't
Have anything better to do
Than sit here
And wait for you
Or whatever it is
I'm waiting for
I just wish I knew
How long I have to wait

burning the candle

I wonder if I made a mistake
By getting myself
Into this
And if it's worth
Burning the candle at both ends,
So to speak
I've gotta do it
At least until I figure
This out
Maybe this is my
Golden opportunity
At happiness

be with me

What do I
Have to do
To get you
To be with me?
All I'm asking for
Is a chance
To get to know you
For you to know me
There's just something
About you
That makes me want to
Be near you
Be close to you
To touch you
Be in your arms
I want to know you
All of you
Good and bad
I want you
Here with me

the type

Is there something
Wrong with me?
Am I doing something
Wrong?
I'm a nice girl
Fairly attractive
Friendly and
Fun
Yet I'm single
Apparently I'm no longer
The date-able type
But am now the
Fuck-able type
Cuz that seems to be
All they want

something more

I'm trying not to believe it
Hoping it's just him running his mouth
Like always
Hoping that I'm more than
Just a piece of ass to you
I don't want everything
Just someone to be there
For me
To care about and who cares
About me
To have a good time with
Outside of the bedroom
As well as in

the game

Boy,
I don't know
What game you're playing now
Buy you sure caught my attention
And you've thrown me
Through a loop
More than once
These past few days
I just hope
This is all worth it

rumor has it

Rumor has it
I want to sleep with you
You want to sleep with me
Whatever
I'm not one of those girls
You just fuck and forget about
I'm the kind of girl
You take to dinner first
Get to know
Then sleep with
And forget about
I've played this game before
And I'm getting pretty good at it

worth fighting

Another day
Another dollar
And another headache
I wonder why I continue
To put up with
Half the shit I do
It doesn't seem worth
Fighting for anymore

inspired

I haven't felt very
Inspired lately
Unless, of course
I can't write anything down
I seem to come up with
Great ideas
When I'm driving my car
And I sure as hell
Can't write anything down then

life less

You felt cool
Beneath my beauty
Gorgeous vision by the
Moon light
Whisper to me of life less
Frantic
Yet tell me sweet lies
About a time
Not so sad

your t-shirt

I plan to sleep
In your
T-shirt tonight
Stained and dirty
And smelling of
Sweat and
Sex and
You

sat in silence

We sat in silence
Neither knowing
What to say, but
Wanting to say everything
It was almost a comforting
Silence as the rain fell
Outside and peace fell
Inside

cool summer night

We were wild and mad
Beneath the moon light
As we laughed in the rain
Cool summer night
Surrounding us
And you kissed me
And like a dream
It was gone

prolonging the game

She seemed so
Free and full of life
Purposely avoiding
His gaze
To prolong
The game which
Was all too short
To begin with

empty & alone

I feel empty
Void of feeling
Thought
Lack of ability
To focus
To concentrate
On anything
Exhausted and
Empty and
Alone

i felt beauty

I felt beauty
Gorgeous poetry girl
Delicious crush
White heaving breasts
Bare beneath my fingers
Sweet dream whispers
Sadly she is you

feels like

It feels like
I'm falling
Forever
Deeper and deeper
Into nothing
And there's
No one there
To catch me

to tell him

She wanted to tell him
She had moved on
She wanted to tell him
She found someone new
Someone that made her laugh
Made her smile
Touched her in ways
He no longer could
She wanted to tell him
That she was falling
In love
With someone else

artist

Can I break
Free of my
Surreal rhythm
Smear the white canvas
Black
Purple
Green
Blue
She appears as a
Smoky silhouette angel
Through metaphors
For raw sex and
Her empty passion
I am drunk
Screaming wildly
Why do we feel
As if
We have to make
Use of our mess
No
Only imagine it
By then a picture is made
And he is angry to hear
She never did like
To paint in the nude
She thinks about how
Absurd
His experiment was
Grown cold
Let us be more than
Your piece of living art

You created from old junk
And shades of color
The canvas
Smeared
Black
Purple
Green
Blue
Appears to turn white
As she screams for him
To know her music
Her harmony
Her balance
After every masterpiece
Has been created
A metaphor for
Raw sex and
Empty passion

grown cold

My coffee's grown cold
Long ago
But I drink it
Anyway
As I try to
Figure out
Up from down
Right from wrong
And what I mean
To you

two words

Celebrate naked
Embrace change
Remember eternity
Think brilliant
Always question
Devour morning
Desire peace
Know cold
Like warmth
Drink champagne
Live poetry

fill

I bring you my glass
To fill with your champagne
I bring you my mind
To fill with your wisdom
I bring you my body
To fill with your spirit
I bring you my heart
To fill with your love

9-11-01

To think that there
Could be such horror
Such death and
Destruction
Here
In the land of the free
And the home of the brave
Our freedom was shaken
As bravery was tested
But nothing can bring back
The thousands of lives
So abruptly taken
Lives that were shattered
Images forever burned into
Our memories
And an overwhelming feeling
That this is
Just the beginning

americans

I watched men
Women
Children
Cheering in the streets
Celebrating the death
And destruction
Of another country
Happy about the bloodshed
And the fear of those
Americans

I watched men
Women
Children
Crying in the streets
Frightened by the defeat
Mourning the death
And destruction
Of their own country
Devastated about the bloodshed
And the fear of our
Americans

times like these

Some people say
Everything happens for a
Reason
That god or whom ever
Has a plan
I find that hard to believe
In times like these

war

This is only the beginning
I f ear there is still
More to come
Whether it comes in another
Cowardly attack
On American soil
Or waging war
In some foreign land
This is not the end
And for every terrorist leader
We get rid of
Three more will take his place
With bigger bombs
And deadlier actions
No, this is only the beginning
Of another battle
In this endless, bloody war

for what

We're killing each other
And for what reason?
For what purpose?
What does this accomplish?
What does this prove?

long time

Drinking alone again
But the feeling isn't so bad
Partly by choice
Partly by circumstance
But a good time for a reflection
Either way
Been a long week
A long month
A long year...

the reason

I'm beginning to think
That I'm the reason
My relationships
Don't work out
And not the people
I become involved with
Someday they'll all realize
That they let a
Good thing go

the one

The feelings I have
For you
Can't be expressed
In simple words
You make me feel
Like I've never felt before
I just hope
I'm the one
You want to go home with
You want to be with
The one you'll always be with
The one you'll always love

for once

For once,
Everything seems to be
Falling into place
For me
And it seems
Like I've finally found
Happiness
And love
Things seem so
Perfect
When we're together
The world's troubles
Seem to fade away
Like we are the
Only two people around

in your arms

I fell asleep
In your arms
Last night
Just for a moment
A moment
I wish
Could've lasted forever

late last night

You asked me to
Move in with you
In a phone call
Late last night
And part of me wonders
If it was all
Just a dream
But your number is in
My call log
So it must have been real
I'm happy and excited
Apprehensive and nervous
And totally caught by surprise
By the whirlwind romance
Between you and me

then came you

I never would have believed
You'd be the one
I'd fall in love with
And want to spend
The rest of my life with
You've come to be
A nice and welcome surprise
And you've got me feeling things
I haven't felt for so long
And was beginning to think
That things like love and happiness
Were all just a myth
Then came you
Out of nowhere it seems
To sweep me off my feet
When I wasn't even paying attention

never meant to

I never meant to break your heart
Just like you said
You never meant to break mine
Seems these kinds of things
Just happen
But I had to move on
Get over you
And be happy
Like you always said
I deserved to be

home

I like this home thing
Curling up on your couch
Falling asleep in your bed
Maybe someday
It will be our couch
And our bed
And our home

still in love

I'm afraid I'm still in love with you
In some way that will
Never disappear
We've been here too long
Been through too much together
For me to forget
The times we've shared
I'm trying to move on
But then I see you again
And the feelings all come back to me

love could be

In all of your
Wildest
Champagne dreams
Did you think
Love could be
This sweet whisper
This glorious harmony
The peaceful balance
Of body
Of thought
Of heart
Of desire

through the motions

I haven't had much
In the way
Of inspiration
Lately
Not only in my writing
But life in general
I feel like I'm just
Here
Going through the motions

beyond belief

I'm tired of being judged
By what I look like
Instead of who I really am
And why is the amount of alcohol
One person can drink
Worn like a badge of honor
On some people
When it really makes them look
Like assholes
There's one in every crowd,
Isn't there?
The need for someone to
Always be the
Center of attention
Is unbelievable
Maybe they're not aware of it
I just sit here
And play cheerleader
To an unresponsive crowd
I guess it doesn't mean as much
To them
As it does to me
And why should they care, really?
The center of attention
Are those in the spotlight
After all
That's what they're here for
To entertain you
Forgive them if they're interrupting
Your nightly routine
Of getting fucked up beyond belief

eventually

There's a part of me
That's almost ready
To be that stay-at-home mom
That I'll probably
Eventually become
With the exception of
The lack of a weekly paycheck
I like not having a job
I like this stay-at-home thing
If only I could win
Some multi-million dollar lottery
And be independently wealthy...

out of nothing

Create
Where there is nothing
Write
Where there are no words
Laugh
When there is no laughter

metaphor

She screams
In harmony
With him
Feeling like a
Metaphor
Deep hard rhythm
Her drug
And then everything
Was black

she is alone

Her beautiful smile is heart breaking
As love dies
Their happy life together
A bright future dark
Tonight she is alone

delicious fire

Champagne paradise
Whisper with gentle desire
Bathe by candle light
Rose red lips
Kisses the soul
Soft honey skin
Tastes of passion like a goddess
A magnificent hunger
Her beautiful diamond smile
This delicious fire
Lingering gaze
Man
Woman
Joined in their dance
Forever

rock groupie anthem

She screams
Heavy with sex
Her song is one
I know well
A rock groupie anthem
Slow rhythm and blues
Wild and on fire
Between the noise
Of
Rock n' roll guitars
In a crowded bar

catch-22

Someone tells me one thing
And someone else says I should disagree
And I find myself stuck
In the perpetual Catch-22
Of doing what's right for me
And doing what's right
For you

marry me

I want you to ask me
To marry you
And live together
Forever

~~*~*~*

what i'm worth

I spend all my time
proving to you
what I'm worth
and for what?

~~*~*~*

next to me

I ache to have you
here next to me
warm breath on my
skin

~~*~*~*

behind

Behind this womanly beauty
a little girl
is crying

dream of her

I dream of her
Weak under his spell
So sad
Void only of his
Love

~~*~*~*

remind me

Remind me again
Why I'm here?
I tried so hard to get
To this point
And now I don't know
What to do...

~~*~*~*

be forever

I want to be
Forever in your arms
To consume you
And be consumed
By you

next to him

The whisper of
A dream
And
Sadly she lays there
Aching to be
Next to him

~~*~*~*

fingertips

His fingertips
Dance lightly
Over her pale flesh
Making her quiver
Making her want him

~~*~*~*

her angel beauty

Her angel beauty
Warm
Soft
Bare
Porcelain skin

she is poetry

She is poetry
If it were
To be
Naked

~~*~*~*

almost famous

We drink
As if
We were
Almost famous

~~*~*~*

my advice

Write drunk
&
Waste time

~~*~*~*

lizards

Weary green lizards
Listen to a myriad
Of discerning truths

www.ingramcontent.com/pod-product-compliance
Lightning Source LLC
Chambersburg PA
CBHW032012040426
42448CB00006B/598